HENRY *Ford*

SPIRIT
of America®

HENRY *Ford*

AUTOMOBILE MANUFACTURER AND INNOVATOR

By Bob Temple

Content Adviser: Bob Casey, Curator of Transportation,
Henry Ford Museum and Greenfield Village,
Dearborn, Michigan

The Child's World®
Chanhassen, Minnesota

7

HENRY *Ford*

Published in the United States of America by The Child's World®
PO Box 326 • Chanhassen, MN 55317-0326 • 800-599-READ • www.childsworld.com

Acknowledgments
  The Child's World®: Mary Berendes, Publishing Director

  Editorial Directions, Inc.: E. Russell Primm, Emily J. Dolbear, and Pam Rosenberg, Editors; Dawn Friedman, Photo Researcher; Linda S. Koutris, Photo Selector; Sarah E. De Capua, Copy Editor; Susan Ashley, Proofreader; Tim Griffin, Indexer

Photo
  Cover: Corbis; AP/Wide World Photos: 8; Corbis: 2; Alexis Rodriguez-Duarte/Corbis Outline: 16; Bettmann/Corbis: 19, 27; Henry Ford Museum and Greenfield Village: 6, 7, 9, 10, 11, 13, 15, 17, 18, 21, 22, 24, 25, 26; Hulton Archive/Getty Images: 14, 20, 23, 28.

Library of Congress Cataloging-in-Publication Data
  Temple, Bob.
  Henry Ford : automobile manufacturer and innovator / by Bob Temple.
      p. cm.
  "Spirit of America."
  Summary: A biography of the man responsible for mass producing
  the automobile in the early part of the twentieth century.
    Includes bibliographical references and index.
    ISBN 1-56766-447-4 (Library Bound : alk. paper)
  1. Ford, Henry, 1863–1947—Juvenile literature. 2. Automobile
  industry and trade—United States—Biography—Juvenile literature.
  3. Industrialists—United States—Biography—Juvenile literature.
  [1. Ford, Henry, 1863–1947. 2. Industrialists. 3. Automobile industry and trade—Biography.] I. Title.
  TL140.F6T46 2003
  338.7'6292'092—dc21
  [B]

  2002151665

19   21   27

Contents

Chapter ONE

A Mechanical Mind

Henry Ford standing next to a Model T automobile

HENRY FORD IS KNOWN AS THE FATHER OF THE Model T, the first automobile that the average person could afford to buy. He devoted his life to building a machine that changed the way people lived. In doing so, he also changed the way businesses worked.

Henry Ford was born on July 30, 1863. He was the oldest of William and Mary Ford's six children. The

Ford family lived on a farm in what is now the city of Dearborn, Michigan. Henry spent his days going to school and doing farm

Henry Ford was born in this house in 1863.

chores. He was not interested in milking cows or plowing fields, however. Henry liked to work on the farm machines. Even at a young age, he tried to figure out ways that machines could do things to make people's lives easier.

In his free time, Henry worked on anything **mechanical**, learning the things that made them work. He loved to **tinker** with gears and other mechanical parts, and he spent a lot of time working on clocks. When Henry was twelve, he and his father made a trip to Detroit, Michigan, in their horse-drawn wagon. On the way, they saw a steam engine coming over a hill. Henry had seen many steam engines operating on farms, but horses

Henry Ford as a young man in Detroit

were always used to pull them. This one moved by itself!

Henry was amazed. He climbed down from his wagon and went to ask the man operating the engine how it worked. Henry knew then what he wanted to do with his life. "From the time I saw that road engine as a boy of 12 . . . my greatest interest has been in making a machine that would travel the roads," he said.

At the age of 16, Henry left the family farm and moved to Detroit to work for a company that made railroad freight cars. Later, he worked for the Detroit Dry Dock

Company, where he learned about many different kinds of machines.

In 1882, Henry returned to the family farm and built a workshop. Henry worked on steam engines and repaired his father's farm equipment. He also helped out with some farm chores, but he was always happiest working on machines.

Late in 1884, Henry went to a dance and spent time talking with a local girl named Clara Bryant. They found that they liked each other and, in 1888, they married. Henry and Clara Ford settled down on the Ford family farm. Clara and Henry had one child, Edsel Bryant Ford. He was born on November 6, 1893.

Henry wanted to build a horseless **carriage**. He tinkered with gas engines, and he knew he would need electricity to power the carriage. Electricity was still new as a power source. In fact, the farm the Fords lived on didn't have electricity. Ford knew that

A portrait of Clara Bryant Ford

Ford and coworkers at the Edison Illuminating Company install a steam pump.

if he wanted to learn about electricity, he would have to move to Detroit.

In 1891, Ford got a job with the Edison Illuminating Company in Detroit, and his career in business was born. While he worked at the company, he spent all of his free time on his engines. He kept his own place to work at the plant and at home. When he was promoted to chief engineer in 1893, Henry Ford was able to spend even more time working on his ideas.

Henry Ford's first engine, built in 1893

11

WHEN HENRY FORD BEGAN DESIGNING AND BUILDING HIS FIRST automobile, he knew that this invention could change the way Americans got around. For that to happen, other things in American life would have to change, too.

After all, building a car and shipping it to a customer doesn't do any good if the customer doesn't have gasoline to run the car or a place to get it fixed. Ford knew that his customers would want to buy, service, and repair their vehicles in their own communities.

So Henry Ford developed a **franchise** system that allowed local companies to sell Ford vehicles in their communities. Having local **dealerships**, as they are called today, also allowed people to get their cars fixed easily. By 1912, about 7,000 Ford dealers covered the country. Ford also worked to build gasoline stations all across the country so people could buy fuel for their cars when they needed it.

Chapter TWO

Racing toward the Ford Motor Company

HENRY FORD WORKED LONG HOURS IN HIS SHOP, trying to build his horseless carriage. In 1896, Ford finally completed a **self-propelled** vehicle that worked, but there was one problem. He had built the vehicle inside his shop, and it was too big to fit through the door! Ford was not concerned. He simply cut through the wall with an ax to make the door wider, and he brought out his vehicle.

He called it a "quadricycle." It had four bicycle wheels and it moved at two speeds. Ford steered the quadricycle with a long metal bar called a **tiller**.

The first quadricycle built by Henry Ford

Although it wasn't the first self-propelled vehicle in the world, when he took it out on the streets of Detroit, it caused a stir. People came out of their homes and businesses to see him drive by. Amazed at his new machine, they followed him around on bicycles. Henry Ford was on his way to great success.

In 1899, Ford left the Edison Illuminating Company to form the Detroit Automobile Company with some partners. At that time, a number of companies were building auto-

Henry Ford started the Detroit Automobile Company in 1899.

15

A Ford Motor Company stock certificate

mobiles. Because the automobiles were being built one at a time, they were expensive to make. Ford didn't look at making cars the way other people did. Most companies wanted to build fancy cars for rich people. Ford wanted to build a car that the average person could afford. To make cheaper cars, he knew he would have to produce them faster by building several at a time.

Henry Ford was a **perfectionist**. He wanted every car that his company made to be just right. So, before any new car was produced, Ford had to make sure that there was nothing wrong with the design.

Ford's partners didn't always agree with him. In fact, two of his automobile companies failed, but that didn't stop him. He kept working toward his goal to build an affordable, reliable car for the average American family. In 1903, Ford and some new partners formed the Ford Motor Company. It was time for Ford to make his dream come true.

Interesting Fact

▸ The one-millionth Ford car was produced on December 10, 1915.

16

IN THE EARLY 1900S, MOST AMERICANS LIVED ON FARMS OR IN small towns. Only about one of every four Americans lived in or near big cities. The automobile, and Henry Ford, helped to change that.

The automobile made it easier for people to get from place to place quickly. Soon, people were able to drive to jobs that were too far away to get to by walking. This brought more people to big cities for jobs and helped those cities grow into large **metropolitan** areas. People no longer needed horses—and the

large pieces of land required for horses—to travel.

Henry Ford's factories brought thousands of workers to the Detroit area. Ford's good wages allowed his workers to live better. They were able to afford more things, including Ford's Model T and nicer homes. Because Henry Ford required a workday of only eight hours, they also had more free time to enjoy their lives. This group of people came to be known as the middle class, a group of people between the wealthy and the poor.

17

Chapter THREE

The Tin Lizzie

WHEN HENRY'S DREAM TO BUILD A CAR THAT the average family could afford came true, it made automotive history. It also changed America forever.

Like his other efforts to start an automobile company, the Ford Motor Company got off to a rough start. Ford disagreed with his partners about the type of cars they should build.

Ford's partners wanted to build **luxurious**, expensive cars like other car companies were doing. Ford felt that the men who built the cars should be able to afford them.

A group of Ford employees photographed outside the Mack Avenue plant in 1903

To make the cars less expensive to build, Ford decided to make them all the same. He developed a design he called the Model T and decided it would be Ford's only model of car. All the parts would be the same, which made the cars easier and faster to make.

Late in 1908, the first Model T was finished. It was different from other cars. Few roads in the United States were paved at the time. So, to keep from getting stuck in the ruts in dirt roads, the Model T was built higher off the ground. The car was strong, lightweight, and easy to repair.

The first Model T car sold for $825. It was not as inexpensive as Ford would have liked, but it was cheaper than other cars that sold for thousands of dollars more.

One of the first Model T autos produced by the Ford Motor Company

The Model T, which came to be known as the Tin Lizzie, was a huge success. In the first year, the Ford Motor Company sold more than 10,000 Model Ts. By 1913, Ford had produced 250,000 Model Ts.

To make the cars more quickly, Ford developed a system of **mass production**. This system brought car parts to the workers for **assembly**. Ford put his assembly line system in place in 1913. As a car moved down the line, a different worker at each station put on parts

Henry Ford in his Highland Park, Michigan, office in 1913

Ford employees work on an assembly line in 1914.

piece by piece. Before this process, it took as long as six hours to put together a car's chassis, or frame. This system was so much faster than the old method that by the end of 1916, more than one million Model Ts had been produced.

As his factories became better at building cars, Henry Ford was able to lower the cost of the Model T. In 1916, the price of a Model T was just $360, and Ford sold more than 700,000 of them that year. Ford had achieved his dream. He had built a car that the average family could afford, and Americans loved it!

21

IN THE EARLY DAYS OF AUTOMOBILE **MANUFACTURING**, cars were built one at a time. Small groups of workers gathered the parts and put the car together.

Henry Ford thought of a better way. He believed that if the car were moved down a line of workers, each of whom did one task in the assembly process, it could be built more quickly. This was the first assembly line.

Ford figured out that a Model T could be put together in a number of separate steps. Each worker would complete just one step, and the developing car would be moved auto-matically down the line of workers. Ford tinkered to be sure the car didn't move too fast or too slow down the line. By the end of 1913, Ford's Highland Park plant had the first major assembly line.

This assembly line worked. Cars that once took six hours to build were being completed in ninety minutes. Ford faced some problems, however. Repeating the same tasks over and over bored workers. Their muscles tired doing the same motions. Still, companies throughout the country began to use the assembly line. It is still used today.

Chapter FOUR

Growth and Decline

A huge crowd gathered outside the plant on the day Ford announced that workers would be paid $5 a day.

HENRY FORD ACHIEVED GREAT things as an engineer. His greatest achievement, though, may be how he changed the way American companies operate.

In the early 1900s, it was common for people to work nine- or ten-hour days and to be paid less than $2.50 a day. In 1914, Ford announced that workers would be paid $5 a day and would work an eight-hour shift. Other companies thought Ford would go broke. Ford, however, knew what he was doing.

Ford's plan became widely known around the country, and it made Americans like Henry Ford even more. They believed that he was a friend to the average American.

Ford's huge River Rouge manufacturing plant

Meanwhile, Henry Ford became interested in **politics**. In 1915, during World War I (1914–1918), Ford arranged for a large group of people to sail to Norway to try to bring about a peaceful end to the war. In 1918, Ford ran for the U.S. Senate. Both of these efforts failed.

As the success of the Model T continued into the 1920s, Ford continued to build a huge new manufacturing plant called River Rouge in

Dearborn, Michigan. By 1927, the River Rouge factory had 93 buildings on 2,000 acres (810 hectares) of land. More than 75,000 people worked there.

In the 1920s, however, other car companies were becoming popular. General Motors was building several different kinds of cars, while Ford was still making only the Model T.

Henry and Edsel Ford stand in front of a Model A in 1928

People told Ford it was time to come out with other models, but Ford disagreed. Henry Ford often disagreed with the managers in his company. He liked to be in charge, and he didn't allow other people to make many decisions. Some of his best managers went to work for other companies.

Ford finally signed a contract with the United Auto Workers (UAW) in 1941.

The world of automobile manufacturing was changing, and the Ford Motor Company was falling behind. Other car companies were selling more cars, and Ford was selling fewer. Finally, in 1927, the Ford Motor Company introduced a new design, the Model A. By then, more than 15 million Model Ts had been built. The Model A was successful, but it was not as successful as the Model T.

In the 1930s, many workers at other car companies were joining unions. Unions are groups that help make sure their members have fair pay and good working conditions. Ford fought to keep the unions out of his

*Henry Ford II (right)
with his grandparents,
Henry and Clara Ford*

plants. As a result, the Ford Motor Company wasn't as strong as it had once been.

By 1932, General Motors had grown larger than the Ford Motor Company. People were beginning to wonder if Henry Ford was the right person to lead the company. In 1945, Ford turned the company over to his grandson, Henry Ford II. Henry Ford died in 1947 at the age of 83. Today, the company is still run by members of the Ford family.

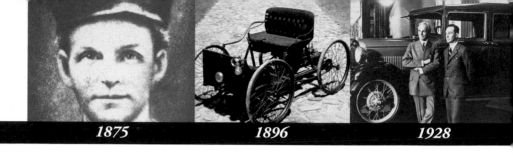
1863 Henry Ford is born on July 30 in Greenfield Township, Michigan, the area now known as the city of Dearborn.

1875 Henry Ford sees a self-propelled steam engine and decides he wants to build vehicles for the road when he grows up.

1879 Ford leaves home to move to Detroit to work in industry.

1888 Ford marries Clara Bryant and moves back to the family farm.

1891 Ford takes a job with the Edison Illuminating Company in Detroit.

1896 Ford's first automobile, the quadricycle, is completed.

1899 Ford starts his first automobile company, the Detroit Automobile Company.

1901 Ford founds the Henry Ford Company.

1903 The Ford Motor Company is created.

1908 The first Model T is launched.

1913 The first moving assembly line is put into production at the Ford factory in Highland Park, Michigan.

1914 Ford introduces the $5-a-day pay rate and an eight-hour workday.

1917 Construction of the huge River Rouge plant begins.

1927 Production of the Model T ends with more than 15 million built. The Model A is introduced.

1947 Henry Ford dies at his home at the age of 83.

Glossary TERMS

assembly (uh-SEM-blee)
Putting a product together is called the assembly of the product. Henry Ford built a new system for assembly of automobiles.

carriage (KAYR-ij)
A cart, or vehicle, with wheels that is used to carry people from place to place.

dealerships (DEE-lur-ships)
Local automobile franchises are often called dealerships. Ford had 7,000 dealerships set up by 1912.

franchise (FRAN-chize)
A franchise is a local business that sells the products of a larger, national company. Ford designed a franchise system to help him sell more cars.

luxurious (luhk-ZHUR-ee-us)
Something that has many unnecessary extras that add comfort or pleasure can be described as luxurious. While many of his competitors built luxurious cars, Ford concentrated on his Model T.

manufacturing (man-yuh-FAK-chur-ing)
The process of making products with machines is manufacturing. Henry Ford had great ideas for manufacturing automobiles.

mass production (MASS pruh-DUHK-shuhn)
Mass production is a process in which goods are made in large numbers. Henry Ford developed a new way to mass-produce automobiles.

mechanical (muh-KAN-uh-kuhl)
Things that relate to machinery are mechanical. Even as a boy, Henry Ford was interested in mechanical things.

metropolitan (met-ruh-POL-uh-tuhn)
Something that is metropolitan has to do with a big city and the smaller towns that surround it. New York, Detroit, Chicago, and Los Angeles are all large metropolitan areas.

perfectionist (pur-FEK-shun-ist)
A perfectionist is a person who will not settle for anything less than the best possible work. Henry Ford was a perfectionist when it came to his automobile designs.

politics (POL-uh-tiks)
The business of running a government is called politics. Henry Ford became interested in politics during World War I.

self-propelled (SELF pruh-PELD)
A vehicle that moves by its own power is self-propelled. The quadricycle was the first self-propelled vehicle Henry Ford built.

tiller (TIL-ur)
A long metal rod that is used to steer a vehicle is a tiller. Ford's quadricycle had a tiller on it, but his later vehicles used steering wheels.

tinker (TING-kur)
To tinker means to make repairs in a clumsy or unskilled way. Henry Ford used to tinker in order to learn about engines and machines.

For Further INFORMATION

Web Sites

Visit our homepage for lots of links about Henry Ford:
http://www.childsworld.com/links.html

Note to Parents, Teachers, and Librarians:
We routinely verify our Web links to make sure they're safe,
active sites—so encourage your readers to check them out!

Books

Gourley, Catherine. *Wheels of Time: A Biography of Henry Ford.* Brookfield,
Conn.: Millbrook Press, 1997.

Middleton, Haydn, and Tony Morris (illustrator). *Henry Ford: The People's
Carmaker.* New York: Oxford University Press Children's Books, 1998.

Weitzman, David. *Model T: How Henry Ford Built a Legend.* New York: Crown
Publishing, 2002.

Places to Visit or Contact

Henry Ford Museum and Greenfield Village
To learn about Henry Ford's life and work
20900 Oakwood Boulevard
P.O. Box 1970
Dearborn, MI 48121

Henry Ford Estate—Fair Lane
To see the home where Henry Ford and his wife lived from 1915 until their deaths
4901 Evergreen
Dearborn, MI 48128